Remembering the KATAKANA

with a supplement on *Learning How to Remember*

Helmut Morsbach
Kazue Kurebayashi
James W. Heisig

Published by JAPAN PUBLICATIONS TRADING CO., LTD.,
1-2-1, Sarugaku-cho, Chiyoda-ku, Tokyo, 101 Japan

Distributors:

UNITED STATES: *Kodansha America, Inc. through*
 Farrar, Straus & Giroux, 19 Union Square West, New York, N.Y. 10003.
CANADA: *Fitzhenry & Whiteside Ltd., 195 Allstate Parkway,*
 Markham, Ontario L3R 4T8.
BRITISH ISLES and EUROPEAN CONTINENT: *Premier Book Marketing Ltd., 1 Gower Str*
 London WC1E 6HA.
AUSTRALIA and NEW ZEALAND: *Bookwise International, 54 Crittenden Road,*
 Findon, South Australia 5023.
THE FAR EAST and JAPAN: *Japan Publications Trading Co., Ltd.,*
 1-2-1, Sarugaku-cho, Chiyoda-ku, Tokyo, 101 Japan

First edition, First printing: March 1990
 Second printing: December 1990

ISBN 0-87040-860-7
ISBN (JAPAN) 4-88996-006-6

Printed in Japan

CONTENTS

Contents

INTRODUCTION

The method for learning the *katakana* outlined in this book assumes that you already know how to read and write the *hiragana*, whose forms occasionally overlap with the *katakana*. Fortunately, the pronunciation of the two syllabaries is identical.

If you are a complete newcomer to the Japanese writing system, we would recommend that you pick up James Heisig's *Remembering the Hiragana,*[*] to which the present book is intended as a companion volume. The aim of both books is a modest one—to teach the English-speaking student to write the *kana* syllabaries from memory as quickly and efficiently as possible.

Following the method outlined in these pages, you should be able to write and read all the *katakana* in 3 hours of intensive study or less, and then to retain them by means of the mnemonic methods presented in the Supplement.

There have been many attempts to introduce Western students to the complicated Japanese writing system. Unfortunately, the great majority offer only one major exhortation:

REPEAT! REPEAT!! REPEAT!!!

Since almost all Japanese native speakers have gone through this laborious process as children, it is understandable that they expect their students to do likewise.

If you *do* learn your *kana* and *kanji* in this way, you may become proficient in time, provided that you are very strongly motivated

---

[*] J. W. Heisig, *Remembering the Hiragana* (Tokyo: Japan Publications Trading Company, 1987, 3rd printing, 1990).

and are willing and able to use Japanese daily in reading and writing. And even if you are one of those who plan to be using Japanese every day from now on, would it still not be much more pleasant to use a more stimulating method than mere repetition?

Most students of Japanese eventually come to read *hiragana* fairly fluently, and many of these also learn how to write them. The *katakana* are different to some extent, since one never writes whole sentences exclusively made up of *katakana*, and rarely needs to read whole sentences made up entirely of them—unless you are going to read old texts or be entrusted with the task of reading Japanese telegrams on a regular basis.

Of course, on first arriving in Japan most people are eager to begin their study of the language by deciphering the myriad of *katakana* neon signs—decorating everything from pachinko parlors to hotels to coffee shops. But because the *katakana* do not figure so prominently in your formal study of the language, it is only natural that it is harder to retain them in memory.

If, however, you learn to make use of what Heisig calls "imaginative memory," as amply demonstrated in his books on the *hiragana* and the *kanji*,* you may be able

- to learn the *katakana* better than with any method involving pure repetition;
- to write them more fluently; and
- to enjoy the learning process more.

This little book also features a Supplement introducing you to "Two Methods for Learning How to Remember." While these methods have been adapted here specifically to the learning of the *katakana*, you can easily modify them for remembering any num-

---

*J. W. Heisig, *Remembering the Kanji I* and *II* (Tokyo: Japan Publications Trading Company, 7th printing, 1990).

ber of other things whose elements can be broken down into small, manageable units.

The *katakana* are arranged here in their Japanese "dictionary order" (*a-i-u-e-o, ka-ki-ku-ke-ko,* etc.) and not in the order in which you will learn them. Instructions at the bottom of each page will ask you to skip backwards and forwards through the book, following the best "learning order." Not only does this prevent you from learning the katakana in an artificial sequence, but leaves you with an easy-to-search reference book when you are done.

The 6 lessons, beginning on page 53, will guide you step by step through this process, starting with *katakana* that resemble the *hiragana* and ending with those that are unique.

Associations are made by using certain English sounds (shared by most English speakers around the world, but occasionally with a bias towards the American tongue) and the standard pronunciation of the relevant *katakana*. For example, the link between the *katakana* pronounced (*ne*) and imaginative memory will proceed by way of the sound, not the spelling, of the term **naval disaster**.

The authors would like to express their thanks to Mr. Nakamura Toshihide of the Japan Publications Trading Company for his continued support and encouragement, and to all those who were kind enough to read earlier drafts of this book and comment on it.

29 January 1990

Helmut Morsbach
Kazue Kurebayashi
Glasgow University, Scotland

James W. Heisig
*Nanzan Institute for Religion
and Culture, Nagoya, Japan*

→ **Go to Lesson 1, page 53**

THE KATAKANA

ア  **a**

You should now be in the middle of Lesson 5. If you are not, go at once to page 53 and start with Lesson 1.

The only difference between *ma* and *a* in the *katakana* is in the final stroke, which stretches out into a long **arm**. In fact, if you look at it, it has a pictographic quality of an **arm** bent at the elbow with a long sleeve dangling from it — presumably of a young maiden's kimono.

フ　ア

Examples

アメリカ	*Amerika*	America
コアラ	*koara*	koala bear
ファン	*fan*	fan; admirer
モヘア	*mohea*	mohair

33 ←　　→ Go to page 63

1

i  イ

The letter *i*, the romanized equivalent of this *katakana*'s sound also helps us learn how to write it. The only thing you need to remember is that the "dot" at the top is lengthened into a short stroke, since the *katakana* themselves do not use dots. The rest is the same.

Examples

アイスクリーム	*aisukurīmu*	ice cream
イギリス	*Igirisu*	England
セイコー	*Seikō*	Seiko Co.
マイホーム	*maihōmu*	one's own home

37 ←　　→ Go to page 43

ウ 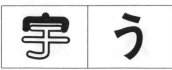 **u**

The only difference between the *katakana* pronounced *u* and the *chawan* that we just learned is the small downward stroke at the top. If you can imagine some foul substance **oozing** from the ceiling, drop by drop, into your *chawan* — plink! plop! — this *katakana* should come alive for you and you will have no trouble putting the pieces together: **ooze** = *chawan* + a drop of something from above.

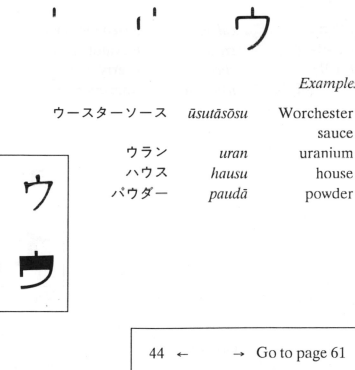

Examples

ウースターソース	*ūsutāsōsu*	Worchester sauce
ウラン	*uran*	uranium
ハウス	*hausu*	house
パウダー	*paudā*	powder

44 ←   → Go to page 61

3

e え江 エ

Let the sound *e* stand for the **air** that fills the space between heaven and earth (the two horizontal strokes). The filling of the space is indicated by the single vertical line.

Examples

エアコン	*eakon*	air-conditioner
エレベーター	*erebētā*	elevator
チェリー	*cherī*	cherry
ウェートレス	*uētoresu*	waitress

11 ←   → Go to page 24

4

オ  **o**

The only thing that distinguishes the sound *ho* from *o* is that the aspirant or "h" sound is absent. The *katakana* reflects this by dropping the final stroke. In other words, ホ and オ should be learned as a couplet.

一　十　オ

Examples

オーバー	*ōbā*	overcoat
オーブン	*ōbun*	oven
オープン	*ōpun*	open
フォーカス	*fōkasu*	focus

30　←　　→ Go to page 41

5

ka  カ

The only real difference between the *katakana* and *hiragana* forms of the sound *ka* is that the *hiragana* again "simplifies" things by dropping off the added stroke to the right. If you stop to think of it, this is really the only way to do it!

ㄱ カ

Example

カー *kā* car

 **ki**

The *katakana* simplification of the *hiragana* pronounced *ki* lacks the last stroke—exactly the same as the form for *ka* which we just learned.

Examples

キー	*kī*	key
カーキー	*kākī*	car keys

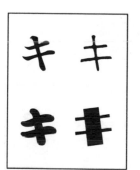

6 ←   → Go to page 15

ku

Take a moment to associate in your mind's ear the sound *ku* with the word **scoop.** Then you can associate this *katakana* in your mind's eye with the image of an ice-cream **scoop** (the flat kind that create slight rounded slabs — rather like the first stroke) dropping vanilla ice cream into your rice-bowl.

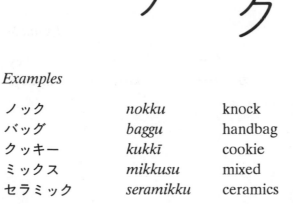

Examples

ノック	*nokku*	knock
バッグ	*baggu*	handbag
クッキー	*kukkī*	cookie
ミックス	*mikkusu*	mixed
セラミック	*seramikku*	ceramics

45 ←   → Go to page 16

ケ  **ke**

The only difference between the *katakana* for *te* and that for *ke* is that the first stroke is taken from the top, and set vertically on the far left. Think of the top of the postbox being opened all the way up so that it can "take the **cake**" that you aunt has mailed you for your birthday.

ノ　ト　ケ

Examples

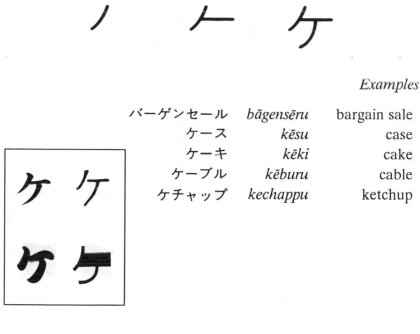

バーゲンセール	*bāgensēru*	bargain sale
ケース	*kēsu*	case
ケーキ	*kēki*	cake
ケーブル	*kēburu*	cable
ケチャップ	*kechappu*	ketchup

19　←　　　→　Go to page 31

9

ko

To learn this *katakana,* first draw the *hiragana* form once and note the same cursive flow from the first to the second stroke that we saw in the case of り . Here the cursive form is changed to block form by the addition of another stroke (making a **corner**, if you will).

Examples

ゴヤ	*Goya*	Goya
コーチ	*kōchi*	coach
コーナー	*kōnā*	corner

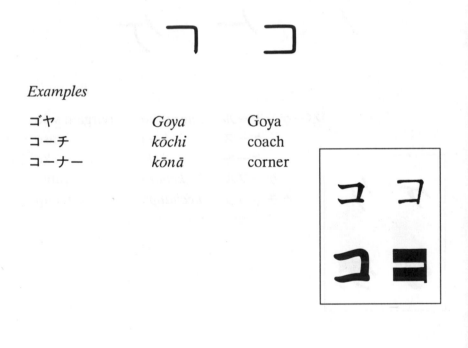

58 ←   → Go to page 18

10

サ   散   さ   **sa**

Think here of the story of King **Solomon** and the feuding mothers for the sound of the *katakana sa*. The first stroke is King's arm, which is holding out a little infant (the second stroke), threatening to cut it in half; the final stroke is the King himself. It should not take much work to see the story in this doodle for the sound *sa*.

一   十   サ

Examples

サウナ	*sauna*	sauna
バザー	*bazā*	bazaar
サッカー	*sakkā*	soccer
サービス	*sābisu*	service
サラリーマン	*sararīman*	salaried worker

27 ←   → Go to page 4

11

shi

Here is another example of the way the cursive form needs a "dotted line" effect for the transition from the *hiragana* to the *katakana*. It is formed virtually the same as ツ , the only difference being the position and direction of the form. Learn it as you did that *katakana* for *tsu*.

Examples

シーツ	*shītsu*	sheets
バッジ	*bajji*	badge
ソーセージ	*sōsēji*	sausage
シャツ	*shatsu*	shirt
ページ	*pēji*	page

18 ←   → Go to page 46

ス  **su**

Keeping our bowl of food in mind from the *katakana* we learned on the previous page, let the sound *su* suggest a bowl of **soup.** The small stroke that drops down from the right will be the handle on the side you pick the bowl up with. A little stylized, perhaps, but definitely a handle.

フ　ス

Examples

スーツ	*sūtsu*	suit of clothes
スープ	*sūpu*	soup
ソース	*sōsu*	sauce
スーパー	*sūpā*	super-market
ナンセンス	*nansensu*	nonsense

28 ←　　→ Go to page 23

13

se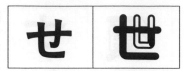

The second stroke of the *hiragana* pronounced *se* is dropped here to give the simplified *katakana* form. Only note carefully how the writing differs, and in particular why the "hook" runs DOWN here, and UP in the *hiragana* form.

Example

セリカ   *Serika*   Celica

ソ  **so**

As with キ and カ, the *katakana* for *so* simply drops the final stroke of the *hiragana* form.

ヽ　ソ

Example

ソーリー　　*sōrī*　　sorry

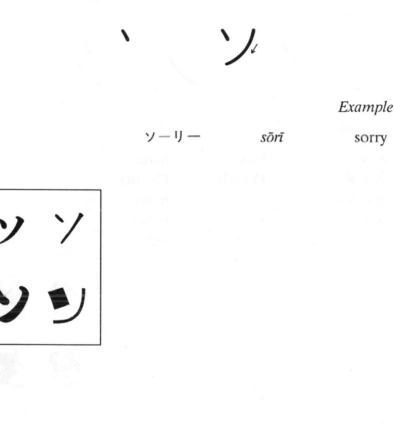

ta

The scoop of ice cream in the bowl that we just found in the *kata-kana* for *ku* is actually resting on a sweet **tart** in the bottom of the bowl (the third and final stroke).

ノ　　ク　　タ

Examples

バター	*batā*	butter
カナダ	*Kanada*	Canada
モーター	*mōtā*	motor
メーター	*mētā*	meter
タクシー	*takushī*	taxi

8 ←　　　→ Go to page 44

16

チ  **chi**

The Japanese word for *1,000* (which appears in the name of Chiba Prefecture, literally, "Thousand Leaves") gives us the *katakana* of the same pronunciation. Presuming that you already know this *kanji,* there is nothing more for you to do.

If you find yourself coming back to this page because you did NOT in fact ever know the *kanji* for *1,000,* you can play with the sound **chief** and construct an appropriate image from the great one-feathered (first stroke) stick figure (strokes 2 and 3).

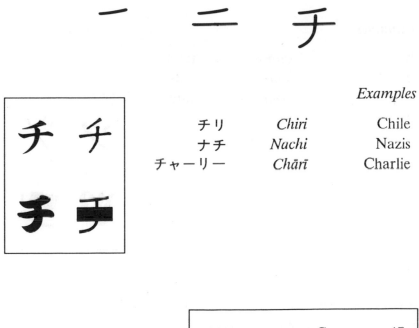

Examples

チリ	*Chiri*	Chile
ナチ	*Nachi*	Nazis
チャーリー	*Chārī*	Charlie

tsu

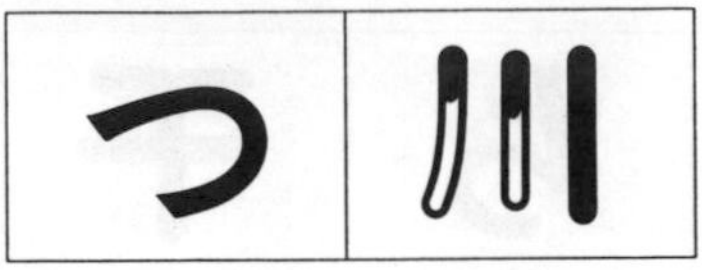

ツ

The *hiragana* form for *tsu* is a single flowing stroke. Try to break it up and you will get the "broken" line effect of the first two strokes here, so that the final stroke can be straightened out. Draw it a half dozen times thinking of the *hiragana* shape as you do so and the transition should be clear.

Examples

ツナ	*tsuna*	tuna
ナッツ	*nattsu*	nuts
キャッチ	*kyatchi*	catch
ツー	*tsū*	two

10 ←   → Go to page 12

テ 天 て **te**

The *katakana* pronounced *te* has been adopted throughout Japan as a symbol for a post office and to mark postal codes on letters within the country. If you can imagine little vertical lines drawn on both sides to join the two horizontal lines. you will have a perfect pictograph of a U. S. rural postbox. Note, however, that the final stroke of the *katakana* form swings leftwards, whereas the postal symbol goes straight up and down. And the reason the poxtbox post is bent is that it is reaching out to **take the post**.

一 二 テ

Examples

テレホン	*terehon*	telephone
デモ	*demo*	demonstration
テニス	*tenisu*	tennis
ホステス	*hosutesu*	hostess

42 ←   → Go to page 9

19

to 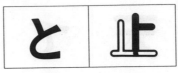 ト

The sound of this *katakana* suggests the image of a **tow-rope** (the second, horizontal stroke) pulling something or other towards you (the first, vertical stroke). Doodle with the form a little and you should be able to see the image in no time at all.

Examples

ヨット	*yotto*	yacht
ストアー	*sutoā*	store
ヨーグルト	*yōguruto*	yogurt
チョコレート	*chokorēto*	chocolate

38 ← → Go to page 27

 **na**

The *katakana* form pronounced *na* differs from its *hiragana* equivalent in that it lacks the final 2 strokes. To compensate, the position of the first two strokes is moved down and to the center. Here, again, set the two forms side by side and the transition from one to the other will be apparent.

一　ナ

Examples

| カリーナ | *Karīna* | Carina |
| ナナ | *Nana* | Nana |

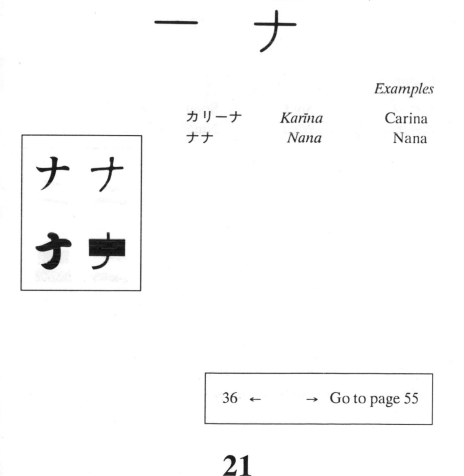

36 ←　　→ Go to page 55

ni

に ニ

ニ

Fortunately, the *katakana* read *ni* is written exactly like the *kanji* for the number 2, also pronounced *ni*. Here again, the only difference is that the *katakana* has eliminated all trace of the brush to give it its block form.

一 二

Examples

| ソニー | *Sonī* | Sony |
| ニーナ | *Nīna* | Nina |

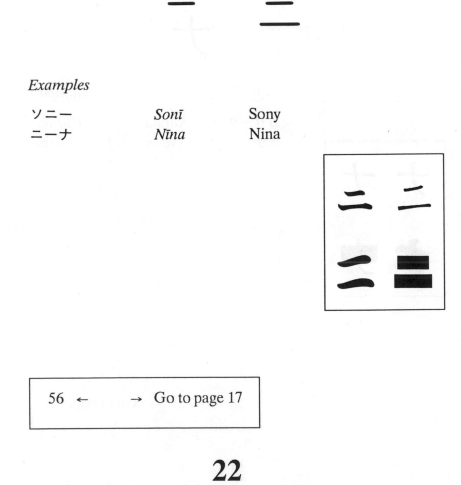

56 ←   → Go to page 17

22

ヌ  **nu**

The bowl here turns out to be the right half of a bowl of steaming **noodles**, from the sound *nu*. The final stroke is in fact a single **noodle** that has slipped out and is dangling from the side of the bowl, as **noodles** are wont to do.

フ　ヌ

Examples

| カヌー | *kanū* | canoe |
| セーヌ | *Sēnu* | River Seine |

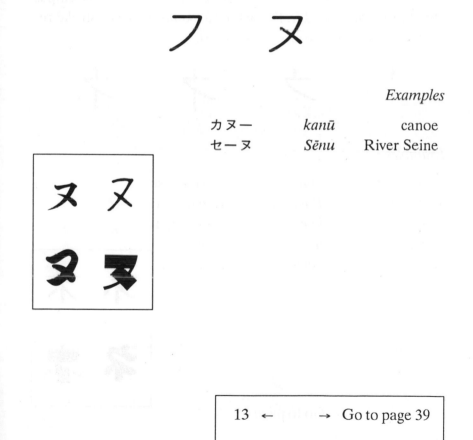

13　←　　→　Go to page 39

ne

This may appear to be the most difficult of all of the *katakana* to learn, but apply a simple trick and it becomes one of the easiest. Let the sound *ne* suggest a **naval disaster**. First you draw the captain (stroke 1) standing on the prow of his ship (stroke 2), and then you add the underwater reef on whose rocks and crags the ship is about to be torn asunder. Draw the *katakana* stroke by stroke repeating the image to yourself as you go.

Examples

マヨネーズ	*mayonēsu*	mayonnaise
ルネッサンス	*Runessansu*	Renaissance
コネ	*kone*	connection
ネオン	*neon*	neon
ネクタイ	*nekutai*	necktie

4 ←   → Go to page 65

ノ  **no**

The *katakana* for **no** is derived from the first stroke of the *hiragana* form. You can also think of it as a single slash, just like the slash across signs indicating **No Smoking** or **No Parking**, or **No U-Turn**.

Examples

キャノン	*kyanon*	cannon
リノ	*Rino*	Reno
ノー	*nō*	No!

35 ←   → Go to page 34

25

ha 　　ハ

The sound *ha* is the first syllable of *hachi*, the Japanese word for
8. It is written exactly the same as the *kanji* for *8*, only in squared
form.

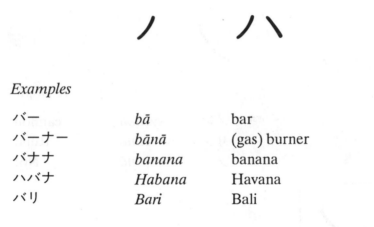

Examples

バー	*bā*	bar
バーナー	*bānā*	(gas) burner
バナナ	*banana*	banana
ハバナ	*Habana*	Havana
バリ	*Bari*	Bali

47 ←　　→ Go to page 48

ヒ  **hi**

The **heel** of a shoe facing to the right should be visible here without much effort. If you need help, draw a long horizontal line across the top and a short vertical line to join the two short horizontal lines below. The rest of the shoe will fill itself in your imagination automatically. Once again, look at the *katakana* form and see if you can find the **heel**. When you are confident that you have the image, draw the *katakana* once with it in mind.

Examples

ビル	*biru*	building
ビール	*bīru*	beer
テレビ	*terebi*	television
コーヒー	*kōhī*	coffee
ピーマン	*pīman*	green papper

20 ←   → Go to page 11

27

fu

フ

Let the sound *fu* suggest to you a bowl of **food**. The sound should be enough for that connection, and the shape will follow from our mental image of that bowl of **food**. To get it just make a mirror image of the form to the left. Once you have that image in your mind, when you look at that *katakana* form with the image of the bowl of **food** in your mind, the blank will "fill itself in" automatically until you can actually *see* the bowl. Once that is done, you know the *katakana* for *fu*.

フ

Examples

フリー	*furī*	free
ブーツ	*būtsu*	boots
ブリッジ	*burijji*	bridge
ハーフ	*hāfu*	half
ハーブ	*hābu*	herbs

60 ←   → Go to page 13

he

The *katakana* form pronounced *he* has actually the same form as its *hiragana* equivalent—the only one of the *katakana* that can make this boast. By themselves, in most typefaces the *hiragana* ⌢ and *katakana* ⌢ are indistinguishable. Fortunately, there's is not too much one can do with this shape all on its own, and the context will always make it clear which of the syllabaries you are in.

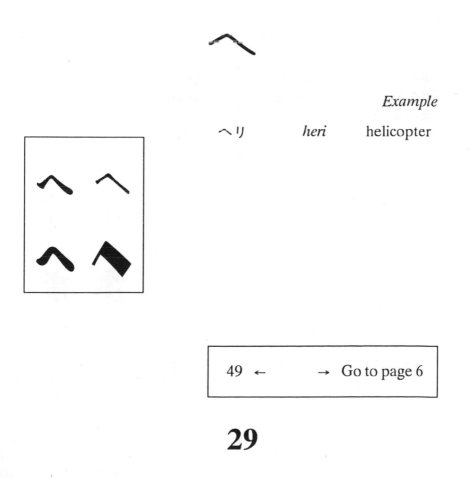

Example

ヘリ heri helicopter

49 ←   → Go to page 6

ho

Let the sound *ho* suggest to you a **Holy Cross**. The two slanted strokes that complete the *katakana* form can either be thought of as two people **ho**lding it up (or the two Marys standing at the foot of the **Holy Cross**).

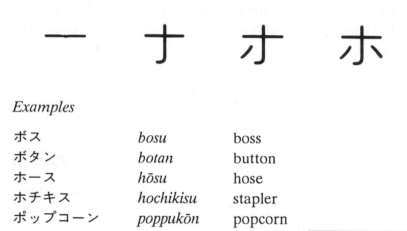

Examples

ボス	*bosu*	boss
ボタン	*botan*	button
ホース	*hōsu*	hose
ホチキス	*hochikisu*	stapler
ポップコーン	*poppukōn*	popcorn

62 ←   → Go to page 5

 **ma**

The *katakana* for *ma* and *mu* are commonly confused. But there is a simple way to remember the difference. Think of the *hiragana* form ま and how it is written. It begins on the left and swings to the right back and forth two times. Draw it once. Then draw the *katakana* form for *ma* quickly before the "feelings" leave the tip of your pencil.

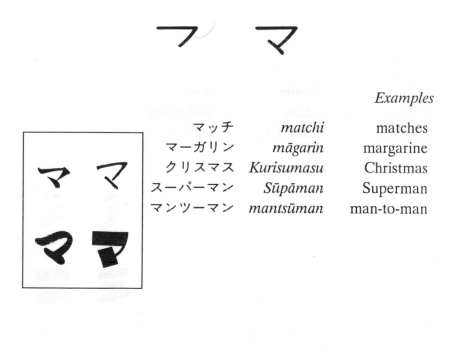

Examples

マッチ	*matchi*	matches
マーガリン	*māgarin*	margarine
クリスマス	*Kurisumasu*	Christmas
スーパーマン	*Sūpāman*	Superman
マンツーマン	*mantsūman*	man-to-man

9 ←   → Go to page 33

31

mi   み 三   ミ

In the same way that the shape of *katakana* pronounced *ha* was drawn from the *kanji* for number *8* of the same pronunciation, so here the *katakana* for *mi* comes from the *kanji* for the number *3* pronounced *mittsu*.

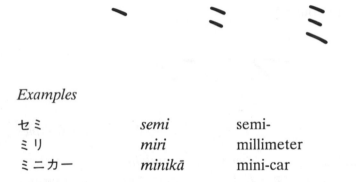

Examples

セミ	*semi*	semi-
ミリ	*miri*	millimeter
ミニカー	*minikā*	mini-car

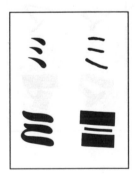

48 ←   → Go to page 57

 **mu**

As we did with the *katakana* for *ma*, here again you need only draw the *hiragana* む and then immediately afterwards draw the *katakana* form. Notice how the final movement follows the same flow for both of them. If you know む, you will have no trouble with ム.

∠　ム

Examples

ハム	*hamu*	ham
ジャム	*jamu*	jam
ゲーム	*gēmu*	game
クリーム	*kurīmu*	cream
チームワーク	*chīmuwāku*	teamwork

31 ←　　　→ Go to page 1

33

me

At first glance, the *katakana* for the sound *me* looks like that for the *hiragana* only when you look at their common *kanji* origin, the character for "woman." But try drawing the second stroke of the *hiragana* on its own and you will find that it leads your hand directly through the stroke order and positioning for the *katakana*.

ノ メ

Examples

メモ	*memo*	memo
メリー	*Mēri*	Mary
メーカー	*mēkā*	manufacturer
メンバー	menbā	members

25 ←   → Go to page 59

モ  **mo**

The *katakana* pronounced *mo* is among the easiest to learn, even though its writing is deceptively different from the *hiragana* to which it is related. Could there be an unconscious adjustment made in the mind of the foreigner that follows the same route as the idea that originally led to the transformation? Be that as it may, note the writing order of both the *hiragana* and *katakana* forms by writing them side by side several times.

If for some reason, you happen to have trouble with the *mo* and find yourself coming back to this page, you might note how it is composed of two forms you have already learned, the *hiragana* Ｌ and the *katakana* ニ , and try to work that combination into an image your mind is comfortable with.

一   二   モ

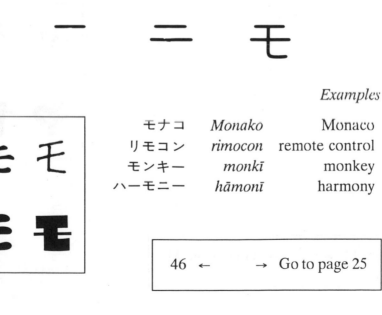

Examples

モナコ	*Monako*	Monaco
リモコン	*rimocon*	remote control
モンキー	*monkī*	monkey
ハーモニー	*hāmonī*	harmony

46 ←   → Go to page 25

ya

Just as with the *katakana* セ , it is the second stroke of the *hiragana*
 that is dropped for the simplified *katakana* form. It you look at
the two forms side by side the rationale behind the simplification
should be clear.

⁊ ヤ

Example

リヤカー   *riyakā*   bicycle-cart

14 ←   → Go to page 21

ユ  yu

The sound of this *katakana*, *yu*, should conjure up without much trouble the image of a **U-boat**. Can you see the periscope (the first stroke) sticking up out of the ocean's surface (the second stroke) for a look around?

ㄱ   ユ

Examples

ユニーク	*unīku*	unique
ニュース	*nyūsu*	news
ユニバース	*unibāsu*	universe

64 ← → Go to page 2

yo

ヨ

This *katakana* can best be remembered as a kind of crude drawing of a **yoke of oxen** walking from right to left, two of them in fact. If you draw little circles in the spaces between the prongs, you can see the ox-heads more clearly. Then erase them, and the form should come to life.

フ　ヲ　ヨ

Examples

ヨガ	*yoga*	yoga
ジョン	*Jon*	John
ヨーロッパ	*Yōroppa*	Europe
ニューヨーク	*Nyūyōku*	New York

ヨ　ヨ
ヨ　ヨ

43　←　　→　Go to page 20

38

ラ 良 ら **ra**

Here our bowl is a bowl of **rāmen** noodles, stacked high to over-flowing. If you happen to like **rāmen** (which is what you gener-ally get when you buy plastic "cup-of-noodles"), the association will be easier. If you don't, you may have to force yourself to eat the entire bowl in imagination before the *katakana* turns into a picture for the sound *ra*.

一　ラ

Examples

ラブ	*rabu*	love
ランチ	*ranchi*	lunch
コーラ	*kōra*	cola
カメラ	*kamera*	camera
ラーメン	*rāmen*	rāmen noodles

23　←　　→　Go to page 45

リ

The character read *ri* is written nearly the same as the *hiragana* り, the only difference being that there is no connecting line between the two downward strokes. You may find it more "natural" to follow the *hiragana* form and "hook" the first stroke upwards, but remember: the *katakana* are BLOCK letters and are not meant to have any cursive flow to them.

丨　リ

リ　リ
リ　リ

If can you pronounce the name of the famous **Rumpelstilzchen** in German fashion as well as the young maiden who needed to spin straw into gold, you will have your image for learning this *katakana*. Look at the shape and on the right you will see the dwarf's little foot with its pointed shoe, and to the left the peg leg that he drove into the ground in anger when his name was discovered and he was deprived of her child as a reward for his services.

ノ　ル

Examples

セール	*sēru*	sale
ミルク	*miruku*	milk
ホール	*hōru*	hall; hole
ボールペン	*bōrupen*	ballpen
オルガン	*orugan*	organ

5 ←　　　→ Go to page 42

re  レ

The *katakana* for the sound *re* is only the right half of the *katakana* for *ru*. Taking the same image we used there of the dwarf's leg with the pointed shoe at the end, you need only think of a running **race** of the little creatures who have only one leg, and not so much as a peg-leg to help them hop along.

Examples

カレー	*karē*	curry
レモン	*remon*	lemon
ナポレオン	*Naporeon*	Napoleon
モノレール	*monorēru*	monorail

41 ←   → Go to page 19

ロ  **ro**

Let the sound of this *katakana* suggest to you the image of a mass of fish-eggs or **roe** as they are also known in English. The only difference is that they are not round but SQUARE — the reason being that the *katakana* do not use rounded shapes but square everything off.

| ❘ | ⊓ | ☐ |

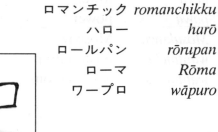

Examples

ロマンチック	*romanchikku*	romantic
ハロー	*harō*	hello
ロールパン	*rōrupan*	bread roll
ローマ	*Rōma*	Rome
ワープロ	*wāpuro*	word-processor

2 ←   → Go to page 38

wa

The bowl in this picture serves in this *katakana* as a tea-bowl or cha**wan**. You know it is a cha**wan** because there is a little red arrow painted right in the middle of it indicating where you are supposed to put your lips when you pick it up to drink.

ー　ワ

Examples

タワー	*tāwā*	tower
パワー	*pawā*	power
モスクワ	*Mosukuwa*	Moscow
ワンタッチ	*wantatchi*	push-button
ワンタンスープ	*wantansūpu*	won ton soup

16　←　　　→　Go to page 3

44

ヲ  **WO**

The sound *wo* is a rather tricky one to isolate in English, so let us take the first thing that pops to mind: **Woe** is me! And the reasons that **woe** has befallen me is that there is a great crack right through the middle of my bowl of food—the only bowl I have to eat out of. Locate the crack, pronounce the lamentation, and the *katakana* for *wo* is yours forever!

39 ←   → Go to page 8

n  ン

Now try your hand at making the transition from cursive to block writing yourself. Begin with the *hiragana* form ん and see if you can't use the "dot and straight line" effect to create the *katakana* sound for *n*. You should end up with the correct shape automatically.

Examples

パン	*pan*	bread
チキン	*chikin*	chicken
ハンガー	*hangā*	coat-hanger
シャンソン	*shanson*	chanson
シンガーミシン	*shingāmishin*	Singer
		sewing machine

ン ン
ン ツ

12 ←   → Go to page 35

46

voiced mark

Written exactly the same for *katakana* and *hiragana*, the **voiced mark** makes a new range of sounds available. The examples below only represent the new sounds we can make from the 10 *katakana* we have already learned. Other examples will follow.

Examples

ベーカリー	*bēkarī*	bakery
ガーゼ	*gāze*	gauze
ベニヤ	*beniya*	veneer

17 ←　　　→ Go to page 26

plosive mark

O

Like the voice mark, the **plosive mark** is shared by the *hiragana* and *katakana*. It looks the same and functions the same, with no difference. A few examples, drawn from the *katakana* we already learned, follow.

Examples

パリ	*Pari*	Paris
パセリ	*pāseri*	parsley
パーカー	*Pākā*	Parker
ペーパー	*pēpā*	paper

26 ←   → Go to page 32

48

─   **long mark**

Before we go any further, it is important to learn the way the *katakana* make use of the **dash**. The romanization of Japanese words typically adds a short dash or "macron" over a vowel to indicate a lenghtening of the sound (e. g., *sumō, Kyūshū*), which the *hiragana* takes care of by adding an extra vowel (thus giving us すもう and きゅうしゅう).

In the case of the *katakana*, however, this same function is performed by adding a dash the length of an entire *katakana* character after the vowel to be lengthened.

Examples

| リ リ ー | *rirī* | lily |
| リ ー | *Rī* | Lee |

40 ←   → Go to page 29

49

THE LESSONS

LESSON 1

This first lesson will teach you 8 of the *katakana* in about as much time as it takes you to read the text. The reason is simple: they are all virtual equivalents of the *hiragana*. Of course if they were exactly the same, the confusion would be enormous. But the *katakana* keep their distinctness by being more squared and less cursive than the *hiragana*. You might think of them a step further removed from the *kanji* than the *hiragana*.

Before actually getting to the 8 *katakana* themselves to see how this works, you might want to familiarize yourself with the layout of this book. Open at random to any of the *katakana* pages (1–49).

- At the top of each page, on the inside margin and in large type, you will find a single *katakana* character. On the outside margin in comparable bold type is its standard romanization (alphabetic pronunciation). This arrangement will aid you later in reviewing: by opening the book only halfway, you can flip through the pages at random so that only the alphabetic equivalents are visible and the *katakana* is hidden from view.

- In the middle at the top is a box divided in half. The outside half contains the *hiragana* equivalent of the *katakana* being treated. That you already know. The inside half of the box holds the Chinese character or *kanji* from which the *katakana* form derives, the form of the *katakana* having been marked in darker ink to show the derivation more clearly. There is no need to memorize any of this now, but you may find it useful in your later study of the *kanji*.

53

- There follows an explanation of how to remember the *katakana* being treated. It ends with instructions on how to draw the form, stroke by stroke, following the standard in current textbooks used by Japanese children.

- The pronunciation of the *katakana* is EXACTLY the same as its *hiragana* relative. The few practice examples that follow are arranged so that you can block off the *katakana* to test yourself. The examples are cumulative, using only those *katakana* you have already learned. Do not skip these drills.

- Opposite the examples and set off in another box are a few of the variant styles in which you might meet the *katakana*, two in print and two in calligraphy. Do not attempt to imitate them. They are given here for recognition only.

- Finally you will see instructions set in a small frame to the outside margin, reminding you where you have just come from and telling you where to go next.

Have ready several sheets of practice paper lined with boxes of at least 1 cm. square. This will help you get a better "feel" for the shape of the character. If you are in Japan, you can make your way to any corner stationery store and pick up a couple of boxed notebooks that children use for practicing writing.

Take a look at the clock and write down the time in the white space below. And then . . .

→ Go to page 40

54

Time: Lesson 1

You have just learned 8 of the 46 *hiragana,* and probably a lot quicker than you had imagined. Above you will see a small box marked *Time: Lesson 1.* Before doing anything else, calculate how long it took you to complete the lesson and record it there.

By now you are probably wondering what to do about reviewing what you have learned. For the time being, let the problem ride. In many students, eagerness to start reviewing right away only reinforces the bad image they have of their own powers of memory. One of the aims of this book is to help just such people find a better relationship with their memory.

Furthermore, by the time you have completed the *katakana* and are really ready for review, you will be running into the Supplement, which introduces two novel but proven methods of review that we feel are helpful for learning the Japanese writing systems.

Meantime, if you get stuck, there is always the Alphabetic Index on page 85 to help you find your way back to the troublesome *katakana.* (Of course, if you have worked your way through Heisig's *Remembering the Hiragana,* you would already have mastered the *a-ka-sa-ta-na-ha-ma-ya-ra-wa-n* order of the syllabaries.)

Take a break now. It will give your mind a chance to clear and help you concentrate better. More important, it will help prevent you from rushing ahead too quickly, which will only slow down your progress in the long run.

End of Lesson 1

55

LESSON 2

Lesson 2 will take you through a mere 4 *katakana*, but it will also introduce to you the plosive mark and the voiced mark—which are used exactly as they are in the *hiragana*.

Incidentally, the syllables that Japanese uses to make diphthongs (*a, i, e, o, ya, yu, yo*) and to double certain consonantal sounds (*tsu*) also follow exactly the same principles in the *katakana* as they do in the *hiragana*. Hence no further mention will be made of this fact when the *katakana* corresponding to these syllables are introduced.

The examples are limited to "foreign loan words" to avoid burdening you with a vocabulary lesson on each page. Therefore, you will notice that even with the 8 *katakana* of the former lesson, there are still too few sounds to make very many examples. So be sure to take your time with those that are provided. As you advance from Lesson to Lesson, you can always back up to re-test yourself on what you have already learned.

Have a look at the clock and record the time before carrying on.

→ Go to page 22

Time: Lesson 2

Once again, record how much time it took you to learn this lesson in the box provided above.

It may help at this point to allay your fears that concentrating on how to *write* the *katakana* will arrest your learning how to read them as well. Happily, the reading comes automatically. To show you how easy it is, try reading aloud the following list of words, composed entirely of sounds you learned in these first two lessons.

Don't worry that some of the sounds are meaningless; it is good training for learning how to sight-read foreign names, which will often consist of just such meaningless sounds.

リニーチ	カナリヤ
ハガキベ	セミカー
パミソナ	リーナー
ヤセガミ	セハギベ
ソーペカ	ゾーミニ

Since the point of tests like this is to see how much you know (and not to see what kind of a grade you can get), be hard on yourself when you evaluate the results. Mark every error you make, however slight, and you will end up being very proud of your teacher.

End of Lesson 2

57

LESSON 3

This lesson picks up 7 more *katakana*, all of which can best be re-membered as transformations of their *hiragana* equivalents. In the course of learning how to remember them, you will pick up two more important skills. First, you will get a "feel" at the tip of your pencil for the difference between the *hiragana* and *katakana* sylla-baries as well as some appreciation for how the transition from the one to the other came about. And secondly, you will be introduced to the use of "imaginative memory" through the images that ac-company some of the explanations.

In the next lesson, we will explain in some detail just what steps have been followed. For the time being, it is better to "learn by doing."

Write down the time in the blank space below and . . .

→ Go to page 10

58

Time: Lesson 3

The use of the *hiragana* as a way into the *katakana* has taught us 15 characters. From now on, we shall concentrate on imaginative memory, which there is not much more to learn about than what you already know from this lesson.

Don't forget to mark down your time!

You will probably have wondered why it is that foreign words often get a "long mark" in the middle for no apparent reason. A language like English typically accents its words by doing three things: raising the voice, punching the syllable, and lengthening the vowel (as in the word *concenTRAtion*). Japanese allows for irregular raising and lowering of the voice, but does not punch syllables or lengthen vowels in any predictable fashion. And since it has no way of indicating an accent mark other than the "long mark," it makes liberal use of the device to approximate accents in foreign languages.

The principle is simpler than the imitation, and in fact there is not always unanimity among Japanese editors on how to render particular words. At any rate, once you have mastered the *katakana* you will find that most transliteration comes rather effortlessly.

End of Lesson 3

LESSON 4

This next lesson takes us through a group of 9 *katakana*, all of which are built around the same form. The method of learning will be adjusted to make use of "imaginative memory." The principles were laid out as follows in *Remembering the Hiragana* and bear repeating here:

1. The romanized pronunciation is associated either with its alphabetic equivalent or with a word closely related in sound. We shall call this the "key word."

2. The key word is related to the pronunciation by means of an image. This image is related either to the actual shape of a known letter or to some mental association immediately suggested by the key word.

3. If the image is composed of pieces, those pieces are highlighted by focusing the imagination on them within the total picture.

4. The *katakana* is drawn while you repeat to yourself the "meaning" of the pieces as you go.

If you are new to this method, take care. But once you have been through this lesson successfully, you will have all the tools you need for learning. Then we can begin learning a novel way to review and refresh what you have learned.

→ Go to page 28

Time: Lesson 4

So ends Lesson 4. It will not have escaped your attention that except for the first "bowl of food," there were no pictures drawn in the book. That is because experience has proved that a drawn picture impedes imaginative memory rather than assists it. It forces your eye to something fixed on paper, rather than set your mind's eye free and leave it to its own devices. Far better to learn to "see" the picture in the *katakana* in your own way than to merely "look at" a picture someone else has skillfully penned for you.

That having been said, it may help you to doodle by yourself on a piece of paper, but try to keep the form as simple as possible and to get rid of the drawing as soon as you can. It is, after all, a crutch, which will only help you to limp along while your imaginative memory warms up for full gallop.

End of Lesson 4

LESSON 5

This lesson presents three sets of twins and one of triplets. These are usually thought to be among the *katakana* most easily confused with each other, but with a little systematic effort you will see how simple it is to keep them apart. If you find yourself getting stuck, don't resort to "brute memory." Simply relax, close your eyes, clear your mind, and let the image associated with the *katakana* you are trying to learn fix itself there. Even so short a time as 30 seconds seems an eternity when your mind is a blank. But have patience and the image will appear in one form or another. Only then will it be really *yours* and not a mere string of words on paper.

This lesson is a long one, so be sure you are fresh and have set aside a good block of time before you begin.

→ Go to page 30

Time: Lesson 5

It is time for another test. To the left you will see a list of romanized words, some of them real Japanese words, most of them non-
sensical. We have too few *katakana* at this point to run any other
kind of drill. Try writing their *katakana* equivalents to the right
(after you have filled your time-box above, that is):

rinīchi	*kanariya*
hagakibe	*semikā*
pamisona	*rīnā*
yasegami	*sehagibe*
sōpeka	*zōmini*

To see how you did, simply compare your results with the list on
page 57 above.

End of Lesson 5

63

LESSON 6

The final lesson is composed of a group of 9 *katakana*, which fall into no particular group but have to be mastered one by one. The whole lesson will be the best test of your progress with imaginative memory. While none of the images is particularly complicated, take great care to give the image time to glow in your mind's eye before you let go of it to reproduce it on paper.

As with the last lesson, this lesson will require some time and effort. Be careful not to proceed too quickly in your rush to finish. Write down the time before you set off to encounter the last of the *katakana*!

→   Go to page 37

64

Time: Lesson 6

If you have made your way this far smoothly, then you have practically laid all the foundations needed for taking up the study of the *kanji* in similar fashion. As explained in the Introduction, the principles adopted here were first used on the Chinese characters and only later adapted to the *hiragana* and *katakana*.

If there is one thing wanting, it is a good method of review, and it is to that question that we turn in the following Supplement on "Two Methods for Learning How to Remember." Working your way through those pages may take you the better part of an hour, so be sure to set aside a good block of time.

End of the Lessons

65

SUPPLEMENT

Two Methods for Learning How to Remember

Trying to remember individual bits of information like the *kana* can be difficult as well as boring. It can also be dangerous if you write them on a page in a certain sequence, since in real life the order is bound to be different. Furthermore, you will want to concentrate on those *kana* which are difficult to remember, and not waste time on those you already know well.

To aid you in this, two related methods are presented here, both of them based on the ideas of Sebastian Leitner.[*]

The first method, a "Game of Solitaire," helps you to remember really difficult bits of information; the second, involving the construction of a "Learning Box," helps you to review at regular intervals what you have learned by the first method.

A Game of Solitaire

Start by cutting small cards from thick paper or very thin cardboard. Standard index cards, measuring 7.6 by 12.6 cm (3" by 5"), when cut into four pieces, are excellent for this purpose. They give you handy cards, measuring 3.8 by 6.3 cm (1.5" by 2.5") each. If unavailable, use thick A4 paper, folded alternately downwards and sideways four times to give you 16 cards of about 5 by 7 cm (2" by 3") per page. Standard U. S. paper (8.5" by 11") will work just as well.

---

[*] Adapted and translated with the permission of the publishers of the original German of Sebastian Leitner's *So lernt man lernen* (Freiburg: Herder, 1972; 12th edition, 1982), 64-73, 119-124.

Write one romanized pronunciation on the front of each card and its corresponding *kana* on the flip-side, along with helpful hints for remembering it. Make at least twenty such cards.

As sequences of Japanese *kana* and *kanji* are best written vertically, and since you might like to continue using this system in future for vocabulary written with several *kana* and *kanji*, it may be advisable from the beginning to turn these cards lengthwise.

Shuffle the deck of twenty cards and lay out three cards on a flat surface with the romanized pronunciation uppermost, like this:

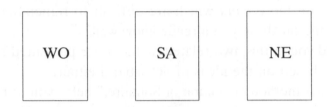

See (only for a few seconds) if you can still remember the shape of the *kana* on the left-hand side of this row (WO). If you have forgotten it, flip the card over, look at the shape of the *kana*, and try to remember it. Then put the card, romanized pronunciation face-up as before, at the far right end of the row. Shift all three cards one card-width to the left, so that they lie in front of you as before, only in a new sequence:

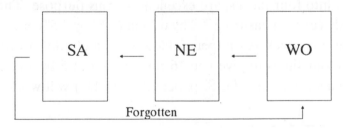

Now look at the second card (SA) — which has moved to the far left — and, if you find that you have forgotten it, move it to the far

70

right. Push all cards to the left once again, which will give you:

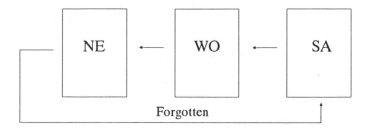

Forgotten

Repeat this process until you can finally remember the correct writing of *one* of these three *kana*, in the present example the *kana* NE. This card is not returned to the right-hand side of the row, but placed one row higher to start a new row. You will NOT have to deal as intensively with this row as with the bottom one.

On the right-hand side of the lower row you now place a fourth card with a new *kana* (in this example the *kana* RU). Once again we have three cards in Row 1:

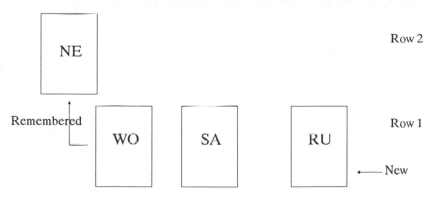

Continue in this way. If you can remember the correct shape of the *kana* on the far left of Row 1, it is immediately moved up to the right-hand side of Row 2. This process goes on until there are *five* cards in Row 2—the maximum allowed for that row. Thus:

71

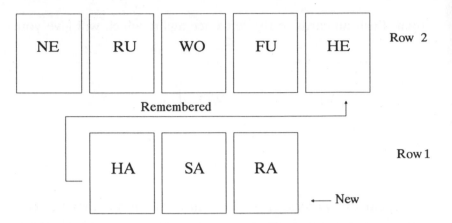

The main point should be clear: kana remembered correctly are placed in Row 2 for the time being, while those consistently forgotten remain in Row 1 to be looked at again and again.

When you now find that a *sixth* card is to be added to Row 2, look at the left-most card in that row. Can you still remember it? If you can, elevate it one level higher to start a new Row 3. If you cannot, banish it to the far right of Row 1:

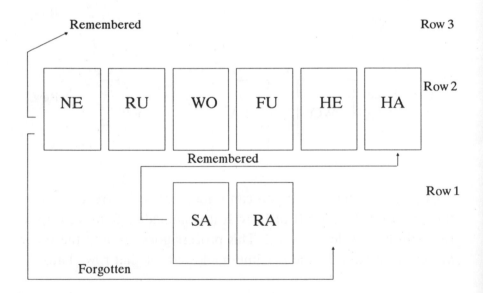

In time (but more slowly than with Row 2) Row 3 will also get longer and longer as remembered cards from Row 2 move up. Continue until Row 3 also has 5 cards. Once the sixth card is added, look at the card on the far left, which has been sitting un-attended for some time. If you do remember it, it moves up to begin Row 4; if you do not, it drops all the way back down to the far right of Row 1.

In this way you can construct a 4-storied "house of cards," each story consisting of a number of cards, as shown in the diagram on the following page. Row 1 consists of three cards, Rows 2 and 3 of five cards each, and the top row of seven cards, for a total of 20 cards. (Even if you are studying more than 20 cards at a time, you need not change this configuration.)

You may have heard of the picturesque Japanese children's festival on November 15 called *Shichi-go-san* ("7-5-3" after the age of the children that participate). This might help you to remember the maximum number of cards permitted in each row, counting from the top downwards in our Game of Solitaire: *Shichi — go — (go) — san* or 7–5–(5)–3.

In the diagram on the following page you see a picture of the Game of Solitaire where all the rows have been filled. *Kana* you remembered easily have moved relatively more quickly to the top than the others. Those which you forgot on the way had to go back each time to "square one," to start their climb all over again from that position. The arrows mark the way of the remembered and of the forgotten *kana*.

In the present example we find that the *kana* NE was the easiest one to remember, which is why it occupies the highest position: the far left-hand side of the top row. Once an eighth card has moved up to Row 4 to join the other seven, the NE is tested for the last time. If you can still remember it, it moves out of the game to form the base of a final stack of remembered cards. If you forgot the

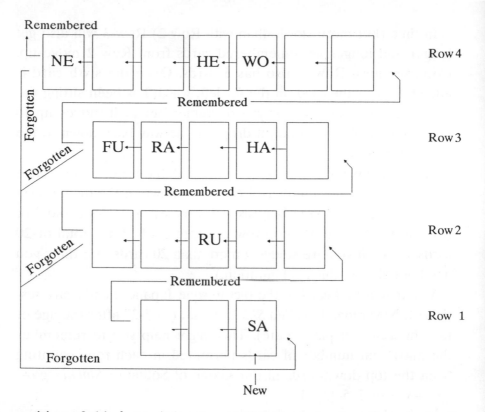

writing of this *kana*, it has to go all the way back to "square one" in Row 1.

Compared to the top position of *kana* NE, *kana* RU is not in such a good position. It seems that you have trouble remembering it, otherwise it would not be so far behind the top cards. The worst-remembered card is *kana* SA. This either never left Row 1, that is to say, it was never really remembered, or it had to fall back down from higher positions time and again.

The Game of Solitaire can end only after all twenty cards have been out on the table. To end, first stop feeding new cards into Row 1, even when space becomes available. As more and more cards leave the game from the top left hand side, the end draws near. When the last *kana* card has passed through the top row, the game is over, leaving you with a single stack of twenty well-remembered cards.

Here, once again, are the rules of the game:

- The lowest Row 1 of the game consists of three cards. Always go through them left to right. Cards you remember move to Row 2, the next row higher. Then a new card is added from your original stack to the far right of Row 1, so that you always have three cards in front of you.

- Row 2 will build up to a maximum of five cards. If a sixth one is added to the far right, the card on the far left is looked at again. If you remember the Japanese writing of this *kana*, it goes up to Row 3. However, if you forgot the information on this card, it has to go all the way back down to the right-hand side of Row 1.

- Row 3 also builds up to a maximum of five cards, as cards remembered are moved up from Row 2. If Row 3 is also full, the same method is applied as in the case of a full Row 2: the card on the very left-hand side is checked, and then either rises to Row 4 or goes "back to square one."

- The same procedure is followed for Row 4, which, however, builds up to a maximum of seven cards. Should this row get longer, remembered cards, beginning with those on the far left, leave the game and are stacked on the side.

- As you work your way through the original 20 cards, they will gradually make their way from the bottom row to the top, and right out of the game. When they are all in a new stack, the game is over.

Unfortunately, you may find after a time that what you learned by playing the Game of Solitaire doesn't *stay* learned. This is where the "Learning Box" comes in.

The Learning Box is an ideal way to re-learn the *kana* — or any similar bits of information that you can put on a card, such as *kanji* — and to work more efficiently with your cards as they start accumulating.

Prepare a box of about 30 cm long, 11 cm wide, and 5 cm high (about 12" x 4.4" x 2"), so that an index card placed vertically will protrude slightly from the top. The box does not have to be constructed from solid wood; a cardboard box with the sides stapled together will do.

The box is then fitted out with compartments, as shown in the drawing below. Compartment 1 is the narrowest, about 1 cm wide.

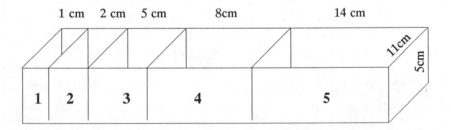

Compartment 2 should be about 2 cm wide, the third about 5 cm, and the fourth about 8 cm. This leaves about 14 cm for the fifth compartment. (Approximate equivalents in inches: 1 = 0.4" 2 = 0.8" 3 = 2" 4= 3.2" 5 0= 5.6".)

This gives us a kind of "mental digestion canal" with five stomachs of increasing capacity. Now the real work starts.

Once you have prepared about 30 to 40 cards as described on pages 69–70, and studied them by playing the Game of Solitaire, take all your cards and put them in compartment 1. Place the box so that it faces you lengthwise, with compartment 1 closest to you and compartment 5 to the back.

Now take out all cards from compartment 1. Look at the romanized pronunciation of the top card and try to remember its *kana* equivalent. If you know it, check your answer and place the card in compartment 2.

If you do *not,* wait for a few seconds. If the Japanese equivalent still does not occur to you, turn the card over, look at its shape, and read any hints for remembering you may have written there. Place the card back into compartment 1. Next, look at the second card, which is now at the top of the stack, and repeat the procedure.

In this way, the remembered cards start accumulating in compartment 2, while compartment 1 fills up with those not remembered — until there are no more cards left in your hand.

This frees you, at least for the time being, of all the *kana* you *were* able to remember, so that you can concentrate on those you could not. The remembered *kana,* stored in compartment 2, drop out of the picture for the moment. This is just what you want: to reduce unnecessary repetition.

The cards you could not remember, now all back in compartment 1, are reviewed again immediately until almost all of them have found their way into compartment 2.

So far all of this is rather straightforward and follows the way most people use flash-cards for study. The items you know are set to one side, while you get several cracks at the especially "tough nuts," which are are reviewed again and again until you get them right. It is *after* this that the benefits of the Learning Box become clear.

Let us say that after the initial review you are left with 3 or 4 cards that you simply cannot remember. Leave them in compartment 1 and take a break.

Now you are ready for the second stage. Make a new set of 20 cards or more and learn them by means of the Game of Solitaire. When you are done, put them into compartment 1 of the Learning Box. During the next day, or whenever you have time to spare, repeat the process described on the previous page. Begin by shuffling all the cards in compartment 1, which include the 3 or 4 difficult cards left over from the previous session. Move only those cards to compartment 2 which you can remember.

As you work through more and more sets of cards, compartment 2 will gradually fill up, until there is no room left. This lets you know that you are ready for the next stage.

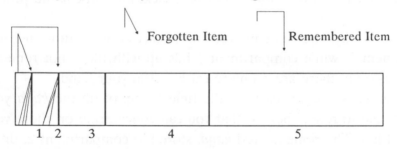

Simply having remembered certain cards a few times is no guarantee that you will retain them permanently in memory. They may be a little more resistant to forgetting, but they are by no means immune. Research has shown that this process of forgetting can continue for a long time. Meantime, as you learn more and more Japanese, you may find that information newly learned tends to nudge out of memory what you have already learned. This is known technically as "retroactive inhibition."

This is why compartment 2 of the Learning Box is only 2 cm wide. The congestion of cards accumulated there forces you to make room, and this in turn gives you another chance to confirm which ones you can still remember after the interval that has elapsed.

To do this, check the cards in compartment 2 just as you did with those in compartment 1. (If there are too many cards there to review in one session, you need only review part of them at a time.) If a card is remembered, it is now moved ahead to compartment 3, which is more than twice as large as compartment 2. Cards that land there may go undisturbed for some time—even weeks—depending on the speed of your learning and the number of new cards entering the Learning Box.

If, however, a card from compartment 2 is *not* remembered, it must always go back to compartment 1, where it will eventually be shuffled in with the new arrivals.

To repeat the main points:

- Make space in compartment 2 when it gets full.

- To make space in compartment 2, review some or all of the cards there.

- Cards from compartment 2 which you still remember well are moved ahead to compartment 3.

- Cards remembered previously but which you have forgotten or are unsure about, must go back to compartment 1.

Once you have moved enough cards ahead to make new space in compartment 2, continue to feed compartment 1 with new cards and review their Japanese meaning. When compartment 2 gets too full again, just repeat the process described above.

Eventually, compartment 3 will also become crowded. Here again, simply follow the procedure to create space, the remembered cards moving ahead to compartment 4 and the forgotten ones *always* reverting to compartment 1. And so on with compartments 4 and 5, which will take proportionately more time to fill up.

The method of the Learning Box should now be clear:

> • All items remembered correctly move ahead one compartment at a time.
>
> • All items forgotten, or not remembered confidently, stay in compartment 1 or *must* return there.

If you have played the game of "Snakes and Ladders" as a child, you may recognize some interesting parallels. There are, however, two important differences:

— When you are *not* able to remember an item (equivalent to landing your piece on the mouth of a "snake"), you are thrown headlong all the way back to "square one," i.e., compartment 1.

— When you *are* able to remember an item (equivalent to reaching the foot of a "ladder"), the rise is only gradual, i.e., to the next higher compartment.

In any event, once the fifth and final compartment is full and room has to be made for more cards, begin by removing cards which you have consistently been able to remember. Ideally, you will not have to look at these again. They have passed the test at least five times and are not likely to be forgotten, assuming that you continue to use your newly-acquired language skills actively.

Limitations of the Two Methods

Neither the Game of Solitaire nor the Learning Box method will be of much help with correct pronunciation and nuances of tone of the Japanese (or any other) language. The rudiments of phonetics are not conveyed through reading, but by hearing and speaking. For this you need teachers, records or tapes. Obviously this can be done formally in a classroom setting, but also more informally — for example, by "exchanging conversation skills" with a native Japanese speaker.*

However, once you have become accustomed to Japanese sounds and gained some facility at reproducing them, you may find these two methods helpful for reviewing those aspects of pronunciation that can be committed to paper.

Some persons may complain that Japanese grammar has been slighted in the foregoing. True enough, but there is nothing to prevent you from applying it to other aspects of the language, or indeed to *anything* that can be formulated as a written answer to a written question — be it a chemical or mathematical formula, the symptoms of a disease, the date of an important event, a traffic rule, the components of a space rocket, or even the kind and number of limbs on a *kabuto-mushi*. The same holds for grammatical rules, as long as they can be formulated concisely as particular answers to particular questions.

A Learning Machine for Everyone

Taken together, these two methods constitute a kind of "learning machine for everyone" with many of the advantages common to computers programmed for learning materials — plus a few more:

---

* A promising start in this line is Paul and Yūko Swanson's *If You Teach Me Japanese, I'll Teach You English* (Tokyo: Japan Publications Trading Co., 1990).

- The methods enable you to break up complex matter to be learned into smaller components, thus facilitating learning.

- These smaller units of learning, called "frames" in the language of the "learning machine," logically build on each other with the aid of a good textbook.

- The tempo of learning and the amount of repetition adapt themselves to your intelligence and industry.

- Correctly remembered items are not repeated more than five times for either method, thus saving you from time wasted on reviewing what you already know.

- Really difficult items, however, are repeated as often as necessary until they are finally remembered.

- You can interrupt the learning process without trouble, even for weeks, without having to start all over again. Those units that you still have to learn remain in the Learning Box, in exactly the same sequence in which they need to be reviewed.

- Making the cards is itself a part of the learning process, and making a Learning Box is far easier than building your own computer.

- Cards are cheap, not susceptible to power failures, and don't go out of style. If you give up your study, they can always be recycled.

... About the Authors

Helmut MORSBACH is a psychologist by training who has been involved with the study of Japanese for the past 23 years. He is currently a Reader in Social Psychology at the University of Glasgow, Scotland. He was Assistant Professor in the Department of Psychology at International Christian University in Tokyo from 1967 to 1969, where he returns regularly for teaching and research.

KUREBAYASHI Kazue has extensive experience in teaching both English and Japanese, and is currently doing higher studies in Comparative Education at the University of Glasgow, Scotland.

James HEISIG is a Permanent Fellow of the Nanzan Institute for Religion and Culture in Nagoya, Japan, where he is engaged full-time in translating, writing, and editing works related to philosophy and religion East and West.

	a	i	u	e	o
—	あ ア	い イ	う ウ	え エ	お オ
k	か カ	き キ	く ク	け ケ	こ コ
s	さ サ	し シ	す ス	せ セ	そ ソ
t	た タ	ち チ	つ ツ	て テ	と ト
n	な ナ	に ニ	ぬ ヌ	ね ネ	の ノ
h	は ハ	ひ ヒ	ふ フ	へ ヘ	ほ ホ
m	ま マ	み ミ	む ム	め メ	も モ
y	や ヤ		ゆ ユ		よ ヨ
r	ら ラ	り リ	る ル	れ レ	ろ ロ
w	わ ワ				を ヲ
n	ん ン				
g	が ガ	ぎ ギ	ぐ グ	げ ゲ	ご ゴ
z	ざ ザ	じ ジ	ず ズ	ぜ ゼ	ぞ ゾ
d	だ ダ	ぢ ヂ	づ ヅ	で デ	ど ド
b	ば バ	び ビ	ぶ ブ	べ ベ	ぼ ボ
p	ぱ パ	ぴ ピ	ぷ プ	ぺ ペ	ぽ ポ

ALPHABETIC
INDEX

85